ROCKSTAR REAL ESTATE INVESTING

Hey Tyler,

Congrats on the new place in Hemlock! Sorry that it didn't work out with us, but I'm very glad that you were able to get it done!

I figured you might be interested in my book. Looking forward to helping you get the next one!

Enjoy,

ROCKSTAR

REAL ESTATE

INVESTING

EXPERT ADVICE FOR MAKING
YOUR FIRST MILLION

JESSI JOHNSON
KYLE GREEN

LIONCREST
PUBLISHING

ROCKSTAR REAL ESTATE INVESTING
Expert Advice for Making Your First Million

ISBN 978-1-5445-1392-8 Paperback
978-1-5445-1391-1 Ebook

CONTENTS

INTRODUCTION

Congratulations on taking the first step towards becoming a real estate investor! We're convinced it's the best way to build wealth and want to help more people understand how it's a viable way to grow rich.

Over the course of our careers as mortgage brokers and investors, we've become experts. We understand property, management, and financing and can break them all down for you into easily digestible bites. It's our goal to show you how to get out there as soon as possible to start investing on your own, or with partners, and to make money flipping or holding (renting) houses.

As you read the tips and learn the techniques in this book, you will understand the opportunities that are waiting for you. With education and experience, the intimidation factor will diminish, and you'll gain the confidence you need to be a real estate rockstar!

JESSI'S STORY

I'm proof that you don't need a trust fund to invest in real estate. My family didn't have much, and they certainly didn't give me anything to get started. I stumbled into my real estate career but was a quick learner, and I became a multimillionaire in my early thirties. I started with no money and no experience, so I know it can be done.

My entrepreneurial career started at the age of six out of necessity. I lived in a nice area, but my parents were extremely tight on cash, which meant that many of my friends had nice stuff and I didn't. For whatever reason, nice kicks (shoes) were a big thing to me for a period of time, but they were unfortunately a very low priority for my parental guidance unit. So, if I wanted a fresh new pair of Nikes, it was up to me. My very first business was selling products to neighbours. I'd heard I needed staff, so I hired my younger sister, who was only five. "Hired" may be stretching the truth since I didn't know I had to pay her. Talk about illegal child labour!

My sister was in charge of "security" and sat in my little red wagon at all times. My business consisted of selling unopened items that I sourced from my parent's refrigerator. A ten-dollar block of cheese would easily fetch me five dollars. Shockingly, this went on for a quite a while. I still can't believe my neighbours kept buying from me without any questions. I guess times were tough in the mid-eighties.

One day, my mother caught me with half of my body in the fridge as I tried to add to my inventory. She took a careful look at what I was doing, and my thriving business soon came to a crashing halt. My sister and I were both very disappointed.

Even though my first venture was unceremoniously cancelled, the entrepreneurial blood was now flowing through my veins at full force. I started another series of self-proclaimed "businesses." I persuaded my neighbours to let me pick and sell the fruit from their trees. It was a success until the entire neighbourhood ran out of fruit—well, at least the fruit that I could reach.

I was always finding things to sell, and my businesses were usually successful. At one point, I "hired" all of the neighbourhood kids to set up booths on the surrounding corners of the block but was soon shut down by their parents. I still hadn't realized that I had to pay my staff for work.

Although my entrepreneurial career was off to a good

start, none of my ventures were worthy of conversation until I reached the age of seventeen. In my teens, I was fascinated by the production of concerts and raves. It didn't take long before I decided that I could do a much better job than 95 percent of the current promoters. I started my own production company, and business boomed for the first three years.

Unfortunately, the government decided to crack down on late-night event promoters, cancelling all "approved" permits and wiping out many of the promoters in the city. This was completely illegal, but the government gets away with what they want. They used me as an example and destroyed my reputation (by cancelling events I'd promoted). My promotions company was wiped out. I was now essentially bankrupt but could not declare bankruptcy. I had lost all my savings, owed a huge amount of money to investors (which happened to be mainly my friends), and now had bad credit. Another business up in smoke, but I was committed to paying back my debt.

I decided to get serious about being a DJ. I'd been DJing house music since I was sixteen and was finally getting pretty good at it. Being a DJ allowed me to travel while getting paid, and I was having lots of fun. I was twenty years old on my first DJ tour for three weeks in Australia. It didn't go exactly as planned, but I loved it and will never forget the promoter who gave me the opportunity. Thanks, DH!

Although I loved being a DJ, it was a side gig and not doing much to help me pay off the debt I still owed to the investors of my promotions company. I needed to do something new, so I started a power-washing business. I loved the work, but it was hard on the body, and I knew it wasn't going to make me rich. Even so, it allowed me to pay back everyone who had believed in me. It took five years, but I eventually paid back every penny, and it felt amazing!

Power washing was a job with instant gratification, but I was exhausted at the end of the day. It became something that I wanted to do to my own house or a friend's place, but I knew it wasn't my future. It was time-consuming, and help was hard to find, so I downsized the business with the intention of shutting it down.

During my slow season, I ended up at a first-time home-buyer seminar, and things started changing for the better. Although I was now twenty, I'd known from a very young age that I'd be involved in real estate in some way. The seminar was a wake-up call that reminded me of the possibilities of a profession as a Realtor or mortgage broker.

I took the real estate course, earned my license as a

mortgage broker, and got to work. It's a very hard industry to break into, so it wasn't easy. I hated my deadbeat father, so living at home while attempting to build my business wasn't an option. I had no money (after paying my debts), bad credit, and nowhere to live. Now what was I supposed to do? How could I run a business this way?

Luckily, I had friends who picked up the slack. Special shout-out to my buddy Tinx and his parents for taking me in. I will never forget what they did for me and still tell the story with a slight joyful tear in my eye.

I literally lived in their basement (it was actually really nice) for a summer while getting started as a mortgage broker. They refused to accept rent or even let me pitch in for food. I would sneak food into their refrigerator weekly, do the dishes daily, and power wash their entire property monthly. They had a very clean driveway while I was there! I attribute a lot of my kindness to what I learned from the three of them.

With the help from my friends, I was able to get ahead and was soon living on my own. For financial reasons, I was still eating rice (with salt and pepper) for a long time, and water was my beverage of choice. Cheese and meat are expensive! The sacrifice was worth it, however. After years of being a mortgage broker—banking twelve to fifteen hours a day, seven days a week—things were looking promising.

As I learned more about real estate, investing started to make sense. Due to my early debt issues, my credit was still poor, so I relied on family and friends to fund my early investments. One deal led to the next, and as I gained wealth and found out more, I created a very lucrative business. I soon realized that from a time-and-money standpoint, my side gig investing in real estate made more sense than the mortgage broker business I had been running for a very long time!

My mortgage team is still in full effect, but I spend 90 percent of my day wearing the Realtor hat and loving it. I specialize in flipping homes for clients, helping them renovate their homes before sale, and helping clients customize a home that they just purchased through my team.

I believe in "true qualification," as opposed to shopping with clients for a maximum amount they can spend on a property. True qualification helps buyers see how much they can really afford. I recommend capping your loan at 30 percent of your income, even though most banks will go to 40 percent or more, so you have funds left to pay down debt or invest.

The last thing you want to do is take the maximum mortgage amount possible. In this scenario, even a small increase in your interest rate can take you over 40 percent, and even to 50 percent, of your income. You have to be prepared for contingencies if you want to take control of your financial future. My mortgage background helps me keep buyers in check when it comes to purchasing too close to their maximums.

Although most of my original clients were first-time homebuyers, many of them are now investors. I use goal-setting processes to help them structure their finances in a way that gets them into revenue-producing properties as soon as possible.

I used the same processes on Oprah's reality show *Million Dollar Neighbourhood*. My role was helping families across Canada improve their finances by refinancing and restructuring in order to pay down their debt faster and increase cash flow. As seen on the show, and as my clients usually discover, you create opportunities for investment when you free up money. Succeeding in the world of real estate investment begins with education and understanding how the business works. There are many different methods you can use to start investing. Stay tuned and we'll share them all with you.

KYLE'S STORY

From an early age, my three favourite things were people, money, and numbers. I was always adept at math and innately knew how to communicate how numbers work in a very basic, easy-to-understand way. By grade three, I was already doing grade-seven math. For some people, math makes sense, and for some people, it doesn't. I guess I was destined to be a mortgage broker, even though I didn't start out that way.

My entrepreneurial journey began when I lied on my first job application. You needed to be eleven years old to deliver newspapers in those days. I was ten. When I applied, I looked at my dad and asked what I should put down. He gave a nod of approval, and the rest is history. I was soon busy making thirty-five dollars every two weeks, which was at least enough to buy some Legos!

In my early teens, I worked for my dad's software company straightening scans for eight hours a day, until I got my first "real" job delivering for a restaurant when I was sixteen. None of it was very exciting, but I'd graduated from Legos and needed to pay for my expensive hockey equipment.

At nineteen years old, I worked at a credit union. It was a unionized environment, and it wasn't for me. I knew it would take three to five years to get a promotion and another three to five years to reach a $50,000 salary. I decided to work for myself because I wanted my action and hard work to be rewarded.

When I decided to become a mortgage broker, it was eye-opening for me! Even in my very first meetings, I immediately clicked with the business of real estate and quickly found my niche working with real estate investors. Having a niche gave people a reason to deal with me as a twenty-something instead of someone older with more perceived experience. Since 2009, I have funded over $550 million in mortgages, growing my volume approximately 40 percent every year, and was named a "2017 Young Gun" and eighteenth for funded volume for all mortgage brokers by *Canadian Mortgage Professional* (*CMP*) magazine.

As I began to experience this success, I started speaking to groups, and my career path took another turn. By age twenty-one, I was speaking in front of groups of more than six hundred people multiple times per year and loving it! The more people I worked with, the more I realized that many brokers in this business simply become order takers, doing exactly what the client asks them to do. Instead of taking this approach and being a "yes man," I wanted to do more to help investors gain clarity regarding their future financial goals. I changed my focus to education and portfolio planning. It's amazing how few brokers ask their clients what their long-term goals are!

I now have an office in downtown Vancouver with a staff of seven to help people just like you build wealth. I try to ask clients the questions and get the answers that lead to a long-term game plan. As a professional, the more I understand a client's goals, the better I can assist them. If I can see where you are and where you want to be, I can show you different avenues to reach your goals. Then, we can create a final system to follow so you won't waste your time and money taking actions that won't pay off.

Understanding your long-term goals allows us to set up your financing to meet them. For example, someone planning on buying one or two rental properties will require a very different financial and corporate structure than someone wanting to buy twenty. I ask my clients to zoom out and take a high-level view of goals and objectives. I want investors to put thought into where they want to be in five or ten years. If you create a game plan first, you'll know exactly what you need to do to make it happen. As Steven Covey, author of *The 7 Habits of Highly Effective People*, would say, "Begin with the end in mind."

THE SAFEST INVESTMENT

We both fell into the business of real estate because we were looking for a smart and secure way to make money. You may also be at a place in your life where you're thinking about the future and looking for a side gig or good investment to add to your bottom line. If so, real estate is a real opportunity. Keep reading and we'll make you a believer.

The beauty of investing in real estate is that it's one of the only investments that you can make using someone else's money. You can leverage this funding and make a lot of money with a small amount of cash, and you can do it in a way that accomplishes your specific financial goals. For example, you can make a quick return in as little as three months buying and flipping properties. Or, you can invest with the intention of holding the property and grow your equity while a renter pays down your principal.

Returns from investing in real estate are generally much higher and more secure than investments in other asset classes. If you decide to buy stocks and bonds, you generally have to put 100 percent down to make an investment. Anyone with available money can have an investment portfolio, but it won't work for you like real estate does.

We all know that it can be risky to invest in stocks and bonds, and the return is not as great as it used to be. The stock market is volatile, and interest rates fluctuate. Although you'll still be at the mercy of market fluctuations if you invest in real estate, the difference is that you now have a hard asset if the economy crashes.

People always need somewhere to live, so there's built-in security in your real estate investment. Even if the value of your property diminishes in an economic downturn, it's rare to see rental rates decline. You have a hard asset, so you'll always be able to produce cash flow. The other good news is that there's never been a ten-year period when average home prices didn't rise in Canada. If you're in it for the long term, you can minimize the risk, and your asset will appreciate.

USING OTHER PEOPLE'S MONEY TO FUEL YOUR DREAMS

We work with homebuyers every day and see the apprehension they have about investing in a house they aren't going to live in. They assume a substantial amount of money is needed to be an investor, and they don't have the confidence to get started. Sound familiar?

We want you to know that this is a false assumption. You don't need as much cash as you might think to buy an investment property, and the cash required doesn't have to be your own. Both of us have done deals where we put no cash in yet reaped tremendous benefits.

A good place to start is your own home. You don't have to own your residence to invest in income-producing properties, but, as you'll see, it's helpful because you can use the equity. Home equity is the difference of your home's fair market value and your mortgage or other liens on the property. When you reach a certain level of equity in your home, lenders will allow you to borrow against it for other purposes.

A primary residence also requires less money up front. In Canada, the minimum down payment for a personal residence is only 5 percent (at the time of writing this book). That amount jumps to 20 percent if you're purchasing a rental property.

Joint ventures are another easy way to get into the market. Friends and relatives can make great partners, particularly if they have the cash and are willing to join forces. We'll cover all of this in later chapters.

We're going to show you how to find the money to get started. The key is education. Once you've finished this book, you'll understand the methods and techniques to make money with little to no capital. Have questions? Just contact us!

ARE YOU READY TO ROCK?

Have you ever looked at the very wealthy and wondered how they got there? How did seemingly ordinary people find their way to such extraordinary bank accounts? We can tell you: 80 percent of millionaires started by investing in real estate. They may have done other things as well, but real estate investments made them financial rockstars and gave them a firm foundation on which to build their fortunes and invest in even more opportunities.

We figured out early on that real estate was the best investment, and we made our millions by the time we reached our thirties. The celebrities in the financial pages did it, we did it, and you can do it, too. Real estate investing is one of the safest, easiest, and most reliable ways to build wealth at any age. Let's get started!

CHAPTER ONE

WHY INVEST IN REAL ESTATE?

Who can invest in real estate? Anyone who wants to be a millionaire or wants future financial security, that's who! This isn't far from the truth. Real estate investment is for anyone who's interested in building future net worth and is tired of being a passive investor.

Passive investors are those who invest their extra income in stocks, bonds, or mutual funds and do nothing else to leverage their money. Although this might have worked in the past, when returns were greater, today you have better and far more secure options. Typically, passive investors have been happy with a modest 4 percent return per year, whereas real estate investments can be over 20 percent when leveraged. We'll get to the numbers soon.

Someone who relies on buying and paying off a primary residence as their sole source of investment income is also a passive investor. Buying a home is a great place to start, but if you stop there, you aren't using your money to your best advantage.

FROM PASSIVE INVESTOR TO ROCKSTAR

Sarah is a client who wasn't satisfied with being a passive investor and merely growing equity in her primary residence. She was making $60,000 a year and didn't like the view she had of her financial future.

With Kyle's help, she got proactive. She figured out where she wanted to be and took the steps to get there. She saved enough for a first down payment and invested smartly in her own neighbourhood. Then, like clockwork, every few years, she would buy another house that needed a little work. She'd fix it up and rent it out.

By doing renovations herself, she was able to save on labour and also found that she was able to increase her rents substantially due to the upgrades and improvements. There was a snowball effect once she had several properties. Her equity grew as renters paid off her mortgages. Every time she was ready for a new investment, she would refinance one of her rental houses and pull out the money she needed. Her portfolio is worth over $5 million today. She's a rockstar!

DON'T WAIT TO BUY REAL ESTATE; BUY REAL ESTATE AND WAIT

Are you starting to recognize the opportunity in real

estate investment? It doesn't have to be intimidating if you know what to do and start with one property at a time.

It's not rocket science. You can build a game plan to suit your individual goals and needs, even if you don't have cash or have bad credit. It may be a little harder, but it's not impossible. There are options for everyone, and the returns are worth it.

On average, investing in real estate is better than passive investment. The proof is in the numbers. Assuming you put 20 percent down on a $1 million property, the return on your investment (ROI) just from having your tenant pay down your mortgage for you is approximately 8 percent depending on your interest rate. Even if there's no equity growth and zero positive cash flow, your tenant is covering your expenses and paying down your mortgage at the rate of $16,000 per year.

On the other hand, if the value of the asset rises a conservative 3 percent, your ROI might be as high as 23 percent. Your return is greater because you are leveraging the value of the property. If you only put down 20 percent, or one-fifth of the property value, every 1 percent of appreciation yields a 5 percent return on your money. Three percent appreciation correlates to 15 percent ROI and grows to 23 percent when you add in the other 8 percent created by the tenant's paying down your debt. For example, if your

$1 million property goes up 10 percent, or $100,000, you made $100,000 on your original down payment of 20 percent ($200,000).

Numbers never lie. When you take the time to understand the calculations, you'll see how quickly your wealth can grow. By actively investing in real estate, you get your money working for you much harder and giving you a much greater return than a passive investment in a mutual fund, which might give you a 5 to 10 percent return in a good year.

YOU HAVE TO LIVE SOMEWHERE

Your first investment opportunity should usually be the home you live in. Instead of paying rent, do everything you can to buy your own residence. You're essentially paying yourself every time you make a mortgage payment. Nearly half of your mortgage payment is principal repayment when rates are low, which is around 3 percent at the writing of this book.

Another important reason to start with your own home is that Canada exempts your residence, but not your investments, from capital-gains tax. For this reason, your home should be the most expensive property in your portfolio. If it's the most expensive, it's probably also appreciating the most. Think about it: 10 percent appreciation on a

$1 million property is a lot more than 10 percent on a $100,000 property, and you can earn it tax-free.

Appreciation is a good reason to own your own home but not the only one. We all like it when the value of our property increases, but the real benefit of homeownership is that it opens up more opportunities to make money. When the value of your home appreciates, you can leverage your growing equity into a down payment on your next investment.

MAKING IT PAY

There are four ways real estate can make money for you. One may be more appealing to you than the others, but it will literally pay you to understand them all.

CASH FLOW

Cash flow is the revenue you realize from your rental property. It's calculated by subtracting your expenses from your income. Whatever is left in your pocket is your net income or cash flow.

New real estate investors often make the mistake of miscalculating their cash flow. If you calculate cash flow solely as your rent minus your mortgage payment, you're missing key components. Expenses may also include property taxes, strata fees, insurance, utilities, and property management fees, which can be up to 10 percent of the gross rent. Every house eventually needs repairs, so maintenance should also be included in your expenses as well as a contingency fund for repairs. Finally, you should factor in the vacancy rate in your area. Unless you are in an area with very high vacancy rates, a conservative vacancy rate is usually 3 to 5 percent.

Not all of these expenses will apply to you. For example, your tenant may take care of the utilities, or you may decide to manage the property yourself. Nevertheless, if you're aware of all the potential expenses, you're less likely to be faced with an unpleasant surprise. It's all a numbers game, and you have to get the numbers right.

Cash flow is the key to the castle because it's the key to financing. When you have positive cash flow, you can hold a property longer, the asset will appreciate, and you'll see bigger benefits from paying down your mortgage.

PAYING DOWN YOUR MORTGAGE

A common reason for not investing in real estate is that potential investors don't think they can buy a property with positive cash flow, or think they have to gauge the market to buy at a time when the value of the real estate will increase. Most people don't realize they can earn a good return just from having a tenant pay down their mortgage for them.

Even if your cash flow is zero, your tenant is still making your mortgage payments, and almost half that amount is reducing your principal. When interest rates are low, principal reduction is even greater, and your mortgage disappears more quickly. In 2007, a typical mortgage had a 6 percent interest rate and forty-year amortization. In that scenario, 9 percent of the mortgage payment went to pay down principal. With interest rates around 4 percent and twenty-five-year amortization (at the time this book was written), almost 50 percent of your payment reduces the principal amount.

When interest rates rise, more of your payment has to cover the additional interest, and less is available to pay off the principal. Inflation is a cause of rising interest rates, but even this can have a positive spin for the real estate investor. During inflationary periods, you still own a hard asset. The demand for rentals will rise, and you're now a supplier. No other investment that we know of will give you this kind of return for the risk involved.

APPRECIATION

You should never buy a property relying on equity growth, or assuming it will appreciate, because prices and values may rise and fall depending on many different variables. At its core, market appreciation boils down to supply and demand, which are impacted by net migration, local job market, vacancy rates, interest rates, inflation, and so o. Once you learn the basics of researching these factors, you should be able to find areas where your properties will appreciate at a faster rate.

Since appreciation is speculative, the numbers need to make sense at the time you invest. Even so, appreciation of assets is where you will make the most money and where seasoned investors realize the bulk of their return.

Appreciation is leverage, and leverage is power. As discussed previously, you receive the benefit of five-to-one leverage when you put down 20 percent. On a $500,000 property, your down payment is $100,000. If the value of the property appreciates by 5 percent, your ROI isn't 5 percent—it's actually 25 percent. Remember that every 1 percent of appreciation equals a 5 percent return on your money when you've made a 20 percent down payment, because you just made $25,000 on your $100,000 investment.

This is where the magic happens. The key is that you leveraged your investment. You got a $500,000 asset for an investment of only $100,000. Your return is not based on the amount of cash you put in but on the *value* of the property asset.

If you need another reason to own your own home, calculate the ROI for your personal residence. When a down payment of only 5 percent is required (as opposed to 20 percent for an investment property), the ratio is twenty-to-one instead of five-to-one. Every 1 percent of appreciation on your home is a 20 percent return on your investment. Using a small amount of money to make greater profit is what we mean by leverage.

FLIPPING

Flipping properties is what most people think of when they hear about real estate investing. Thanks to television, buying and renovating distressed properties has surged in popularity due to the "before and after" wow factor. Although fun to watch, it usually doesn't make financial sense to blow out walls and redesign the floor plan.

If you're interested in flipping properties, look for the home that needs a simple, cosmetic renovation in order to make it more livable—and more marketable. This is called a lipstick upgrade. Most homeowners who paint and replace their hardwood floors before selling wonder why they waited so long. Little changes make a big difference! You want to give buyers what they are looking for without breaking the bank.

Making money with a flip starts with the deal at the front

end. You have to find the right property that can be renovated for the right amount. For example, if you can buy a property for $200,000 that you can sell for $300,000, and it only requires $30,000 in renovations, you're in the ballpark. As a general rule, renovations should never cost more than 20 percent of the property value. Your goal is to increase the asset's value by a number that's greater than the amount of money you're putting in. In this example, your $30,000 is working for you like it's $100,000.

THE ACTIVE INVESTMENT

If you want to have control over your investments, it's time to move from being a passive investor to getting active. Real estate is one of the best ways to actively invest in your financial future.

Buying property can make money for you in four different ways: generating cash flow, mortgage pay down, passive appreciation, or active appreciation when you renovate and flip distressed properties for quick cash. It's not a one-size-fits-all approach, and one investment may benefit you in several ways. Regardless of the payoff, one rule remains true: the longer you hold the asset, the more equity you control, and the more leverage you have.

Real estate is one of the only investments where you can gain control of valuable moneymaking assets with very little investment of your own. The bank isn't going to turn over the keys unless you have some amount of "skin in the game," however, so you'll have to find a way to come up with the cash. If you don't have the capital to get started, keep reading. In the following chapters, we will show you several ways to find the financing to fund your dreams.

CHAPTER TWO

BORROWING $100,000 FROM YOURSELF

Before you start looking for your first investment property, it's a good idea to get your financing in place. Investment deals can happen quickly, and you don't have time to waste trying to find the money when other investors are ready and able to make the deal.

You have to have money to buy real estate, but as we've discussed, it doesn't have to be your own. The first step is figuring out how much money will be required. You need cash for a down payment, money for renovations if necessary, and funds for closing costs.

In Canada, the required down payment on an investment property is 20 percent of the purchase price, and closing costs are approximately 1.5 percent. The closing costs may include property-transfer tax, legal fees, appraisal fees, and so on. One and a half percent is a healthy amount to budget, although closing costs will fluctuate, because every situation is unique.

Estimating renovation costs can be a little trickier. Although this is rare, we've been burned when poor estimates created cost overruns. Using the wrong contractor can be a nightmare and easily cause your budget to double or more. Avoid the problem by doing your research, speaking with the contractor's past clients, and testing them out with a small project before giving them the big one.

Similarly, if you buy a property sight unseen, make sure your agent and contractor are reliable and able to assess the cost of a reasonable renovation. The ideal situation, and the safer one, is to go to the property with your contractor(s) and get a quote or two that you can rely on.

Weather can also cause huge delays in the completion of projects. One of our projects closed in January and was going to be a quick flip, but we hadn't counted on working during the wettest, snowiest winter in a decade. The property was on a hill and couldn't be accessed due to the icy conditions. Once the snow melted, the area turned into a swampy mess. We couldn't work outside for months, couldn't fix the exterior, and couldn't lay the concrete needed for the driveway. While you can't control the weather, you have to be aware of and try to be prepared for unpredictable factors that might derail your progress and decrease your profits.

As a new investor, start with properties that have only cosmetic issues, as opposed to houses with more fundamental problems. If you start ripping out walls, you may find very expensive surprises. Keep in mind that a buyer won't see new insulation or wiring and will be much less likely to pay for them. They will see the new kitchen, new flooring, and stylish light fixtures, however. Be smart about your renovations, and look for ways to get more bang for your buck. Go for low expense and high impact.

THE BEST LENDER—YOU!

Once you determine the approximate amount you need, it's time to secure funding. One of the best ways to get money for your first real estate investment is to borrow it from yourself. More specifically, look to the equity in your own home as a source of capital.

Leveraging your home equity is possible if you own your

residence and you've paid down the mortgage enough that a bank will let you pull cash out. There are a few caveats. In Canada, you must have greater than 20 percent equity in your home to pull out equity for another property. If you meet that requirement, you can usually get a line of credit for 80 percent of the property's current value, minus the amount of your current mortgage balance.

For example, if your home's value is $500,000 and you currently owe $300,000, you can pull out the difference between what you currently owe—$300,000—and 80 percent of the home's value—$400,000. In this case, you could get a credit line for $100,000 and use it for your next purchase.

A credit line is a good idea because the payment is interest-only and there's no prepayment penalty if you pay it off early. A smaller payment gives you a higher level of cash flow, and the interest cost is tax-deductible if you're using the money for investment purposes. If it's a re-advanceable line, you can use the money over and over again, even to purchase multiple properties.

Most lenders don't offer a line of credit (LOC), but it's possible to find one that does. If you think investing is in your future, start with a mortgage lender that can provide a line of credit when the time is right.

There are many different line-of-credit products, and they aren't all created equal. To find the right product for your situation, seek advice from a mortgage broker who can provide personalized options.

One of the best products is a re-advanceable line of credit. Every mortgage payment you make will pay off a portion of the principal and a portion of the interest. With a re-advanceable LOC, the amount of principal you pay off directly opens up access to more capital. For example, if you pay down your mortgage by $50,000 in one year, that amount is now available to you as a line of credit.

You don't have to decide whether to save up for an investment or pay down your mortgage, because you can do both. You can pay down your mortgage as quickly as possible and open up a tax-free avenue for re-borrowing the money.

THE TAX-DEDUCTIBLE MORTGAGE

The Smith Maneuver is a strategy that can turn your mortgage into a tax advantage. In Canada, if you borrow money for an investment, you can deduct the interest you pay on the loan. So if you borrow $100,000 at 10 percent interest, you get to claim that 10 percent as an income tax deduction.

If you use a re-advanceable line of credit on your primary mortgage in order to invest, you essentially turn your mortgage into an interest-free loan. Here's how it works: you use the equity in your home as a loan to invest in an income-producing property, and then use the tax benefits to make additional mortgage payments on the personal, non-tax-deductible portion.

As you pay down your personal mortgage, your line of credit increases. You take out more money to invest, which generates more income to pay down your mortgage. The snowball effect allows you to convert all your personal residence into a tax-deductible mortgage.

Cash-damming is a variation of the Smith Maneuver. It employs the same technique, using business expenses as opposed to income-producing investments. A small business can use a line of credit on a personal residence to pay for tax-deductible business expenses, and then use the increased business cash flow to pay down the mortgage. The results are the same: the traditionally non-deductible mortgage becomes an interest-free loan.

Consult your tax professional for more information about how these techniques might work for your individual situation.

MOVING AHEAD

The first step to rockstar real estate investing is to investigate a line of credit on your primary residence. Borrowing from yourself, using the equity in your home, is an easy way to fund income-producing properties and can convert your mortgage into a tax-free loan for all your investments.

Consult a mortgage broker and your tax specialist to find the perfect LOC product to meet your goals. If an LOC is not available to you, there are other options. The next chapter will show how other people's money can help you finance your first deal.

CHAPTER THREE

BORROW $100,000 FROM A FRIEND

Assuming you don't have 100 percent of the cash required, the traditional route to buying a house is to save up a down payment and borrow the rest from a mortgage lender. As noted in the last chapter, however, there are ways to borrow from yourself using a line of credit to access the equity in your primary residence.

Sounds easy enough, right? But what if you don't have the money for a down payment, can't finance the down payment and the renovations, can't use your home equity, or don't yet own your own home?

ANOTHER OPTION

Potential buyers who lack the usual means of funding their investments may think there's no way to overcome these seemingly insurmountable hurdles. They resign themselves to staying out of real estate until they get some money—perhaps, they think, from an inheritance or winning the lottery. In reality, a more likely scenario is they'll wait to invest in real estate after years of saving—a tough, time-consuming road.

Luckily, there's another option for the rockstar real estate investor: borrow money from your friends. We both started our real estate careers in this way. Both of us had friends or relatives lend us money to help with the down payment on some of our first investments.

JESSI'S STORY

The first property I bought wasn't for investment. It was a condo for me to call home. I saved the 10 percent down payment when I was twenty-five and sold it later in life for a profit of over $100,000.

The first major investment deal I made was a property worth approximately $500,000. I had some cash saved from my business as well as equity in my existing home that I was able to withdraw. Unfortunately, it wasn't enough to buy the house and do all of the renovations that were needed.

I followed my own advice and borrowed the rest from a friend. He came into the deal and brought $100,000 that he secured in the form of a second mortgage on the property. The investment was incredibly secure from his point of view. I paid him 5 percent on an annual basis as well as a small lender fee. Five percent was a very good deal for me, but he was a close friend and did well from the lender fee since the funds returned so fast. He had his money back in three months and was extremely happy with the deal.

In fact, he was so pleased with the result that he wanted a piece of the action. He said he would still provide money for some of my investment deals, but he wanted to learn the business and be actively involved in the projects. I still own many properties with him to this day, and we are actively flipping homes together on a regular basis.

KYLE'S STORY

My first real estate purchase was also my primary residence. Like Jessi, I saved up the money for the down payment and bought it myself. The only difference is that I was nineteen.

My first investment deal was a $1.15 million purchase. For a deal of that size, I needed a partner and started actively seeking someone who could bring the money I needed. I found a joint venture partner at a real estate conference where we exchanged information and discussed some potential properties. Once I decided on the best deal and had an accepted offer, I prepared a cash-flow analysis and synopsis that I sent to a handful of investors, including my new contact from the business event. He brought $300,000 to the table, covering the down payment and closing costs. We had a deal!

The moral of my story is that you can't be afraid to put yourself out there at real estate networking events. You can meet like-minded people, and there will be opportunities to borrow money or collaborate. They may not be your friends immediately, but they may turn out to be great partners.

If you decide to join groups or attend events centered around real estate investment, I'll offer one caveat: be careful at events where they are trying to sell you something. It's fine to pay to attend an event and learn from expert speakers, but you shouldn't be paying to hear a sales pitch. The information you need is available to you without having to pay thousands of dollars for someone's program or system. In fact, all you need is right here in this book!

CREATING YOUR REAL ESTATE NETWORK

Once you decide you're ready and willing to approach your friends for money, it's time to start building a real estate network. You may be surprised by how many of your smart, go-getter friends are open to the moderate risk that real estate offers.

Identify the people in your personal and professional circles with whom you would like to work and who might want to grow a business with you. Each person in your network should have a particular strength that they bring to the table. Someone may bring the down payment or be able to qualify for the mortgage. Someone may be good at finding properties. Someone may be skilled at managing the project.

Your first goal is to build a supportive network of a few friends interested in real estate. A good approach is simply to share that you have some amazing opportunities coming up that will make money. Let them know you've done your research and checked out some properties. Maybe give them a copy of this book so they can get educated like you.

Your network should give you guidance, offer experience, and be a place to bounce ideas around. Regular meetings with your group of like-minded investors should be a place to exchange real estate opportunities. You want the people in your group to be successful and work-obsessed (especially if you are), but they don't have to be rich. There are probably friends in your circle who have equity in their homes but never thought to take it out. Most people don't have $100,000 sitting around, but many have untapped equity.

Although the risk in real estate investing is moderate, it's still risk. Choose partners who are not afraid of the deal and everything that comes with it. Your project will be much easier if your partner isn't constantly worrying about when and if it will be finished. Don't be afraid of risk. *When you do things that the average person won't do, you will reach a level that the average person can't achieve.*

THE BIG ASK

Are you wondering exactly how to approach your network for money? It's not every day you ask a friend to do something of such significant impact, so some ways are definitely better than others. For example, we don't recommend walking up to a potential partner and saying, "I need $100,000." How would *you* react?

First, you have to build trust. The reason we can approach our network in the way stated above is because we've proven ourselves. Over time, and numerous deals, we've been able to show our partners that we're a good risk. They know that if they lend us money, they will get it back and realize a great return on their investment.

One of the best ways to build trust is to start small—small amounts of money, small projects. Then, act professionally. Don't simply ask for the money; make the pitch as if you were talking to a bank. If someone is considering giving you money, they want to know they are dealing with a professional, regardless of your age.

Professionalism isn't just shown in the way you present the opportunity; it's in the way you present yourself. At all times, you are a walking advertisement for yourself and your business. *You never know if the person who just got in the elevator with you is the custodian or the CEO.* If you carry yourself well and are consistent in your professionalism, it won't matter, because everyone will see you at your best.

Even though you may be dealing with friends or family,

always memorialize the agreement in writing and get it notarized. Some of the worst joint ventures we've seen have been when friends, families, and neighbours are involved, because it's more likely that they will have a "handshake deal" instead of a formal agreement. Use a contract to discuss the intentions of the investment, under what parameters a sale will occur, and what will happen if partners disagree. The clearer the terms of your contract, the less likely it is that you will have problems later.

Usually, a bare trust or simple contract is all you need. Once you have one drawn up by a lawyer, you can use it as a template for all of your deals, but each transaction or deal will require custom alterations.

PUTTING TRUST IN A ROCKSTAR

Depending on your age, lenders will often make judgments regarding your financial ability to repay a loan. So how was Jessi able to borrow $100,000 at the age of twenty?

It was quite the feat, but I didn't start at that level. Although my first loans weren't in real estate, the same principles apply. I was able to borrow $100,000 at the age of twenty because I had already established trust in my network. I started small and built from there.

I started very early hosting events and throwing concerts. I was eighteen, and I needed to borrow $5,000. I was able to borrow this small amount by setting a hefty interest rate of 25 percent and personally guaranteeing the loan. Then I paid it back in two months.

All of my events sold out, and as they got bigger and bigger, so did the amount of money I needed to run them. The first time I had to borrow a large amount, I decided to treat the investor as I would treat a bank. I did the research, created a proposal, and presented a lucrative deal with favourable terms. I was able to grow the business because my investors made money and were treated well.

At that time, I was an extremely high risk. To compensate for the risk, I was willing to guarantee the loans and pay much higher interest rates. Whether you like it or not, if you don't have credit with investors, the rates are substantially higher.

By starting small and building on small successes, I also built a relationship of trust with my investors. At the age of twenty, I had almost twenty successful loans under my belt. Despite my age, I had proven myself, and investors wrote the check for $100,000 for my partner and me.

WHY NOT?

Instead of asking why someone would give you money, your pitch should be so good that the question becomes "why *wouldn't* an investor give you a loan?"

The best way to pitch to an investor is with a concise business plan that includes a cash-flow analysis and deal synopsis. Most investors understand numbers, so be realistic and always underestimate potential revenue. You will easily scare off potential investors if your numbers are unrealistic. It may also be helpful to send investors your spreadsheets, so they can see how you reached your numbers and can easily input their own if they disagree.

There's a lot of money out there that is just waiting for a good investment. With the right pitch, it's not unrealistic to think that the good investment is you.

If an investor can find their own deal and make 20 percent, they would never do the deal with you and have to split that 20 percent down the middle. The scenario changes significantly if you are finding the deals with the potential for the investor to split a 50 percent return on the investment. Any savvy investor would jump at the opportunity to make a 25 percent return on their money and have someone else manage the project. You just have to find the deals that are better investments than what investors could find on their own.

A FRIEND IN NEED...

In the world of real estate investing, you need access to money. Sometimes, banks will provide it, but your friends and acquaintances may be a better bet in the beginning.

At least, they may be the path of least resistance.

Build a network of like-minded people based on trust (and lucrative terms), and leverage it to access big money in the short term. Start small and be professional in everything you do, and you will create an environment where people want you to ask them for money.

The more deals you make, the easier it becomes to borrow what you need. Sometimes, you may not make the money out of the deal that you wanted, but that's a small price to pay for getting the experience and building the kind of trust that gets you to $100,000 or more.

CHAPTER FOUR

NO APPROVAL?
NO PROBLEM

Occasionally, real estate investors will need a mortgage. You may not have the cash or be able to use a line of credit from another property, or you may simply appreciate the leverage that a mortgage brings.

THE PROBLEM WITH MORTGAGES

One of the best things about investing in real estate is the leverage, or using someone else's money to make money for yourself. A mortgage allows you to stay liquid and borrow what you need at a low interest rate in order to realize a higher rate of return.

Unfortunately, traditional mortgages are hard to get,

and the difficulty only increases if you are self-employed and using stated income. Even if you've saved the down payment, you won't qualify for a traditional mortgage without proof of the necessary income for at least two years. You will need to complete two full taxation years with enough claimed net income to qualify and show your income taxes with zero balance owing. Although there are special programs that may allow for a lower taxable income to qualify if you are self-employed, those programs have become much scarcer since the subprime crisis in 2008.

Before you throw in the towel, however, there is another way to leverage your investment if you can't qualify for a traditional mortgage or get the lowest interest rates. You can still get the money you need from private lending.

Private lending may be an individual or may be a mortgage investment corporation, but the general idea is that the lender cares more about the property than the borrower. As long as the property supports the investment, you aren't required to qualify on the basis of your income.

Because there is a higher risk, the private lender will charge you a higher mortgage interest rate, as well as an additional lender fee. The property still secures the loan, but the lender charges you more to balance his lack of knowledge regarding your ability to make the payments.

Although it's common for buyers to get hung up on interest rate, avoid the trap! Interest rates are only part of the greater equation that makes up the entire deal. This is just a cost of doing business, which is fine as long as the numbers make sense.

For example, you may have an amazing flip opportunity that will make you $100,000. Using private money, you find out your interest will be three times more than you expected, $30,000 instead of $10,000. Instead of balking at the increased rate you have to pay, try to look at it as the cost of doing business. You'll still have a profit of $70,000 at the end of the day. It may be $20,000 less than you expected, but not a bad payday! The $70,000 in profit would not have happened without the private lending.

Don't focus solely on the interest rate. Look at the whole deal and the total cost of the project over time. The most important thing is getting the money. It's a numbers game, and if the deal has enough profit to make it work, the rate (and/or fee) doesn't matter. As long as you remember to factor in higher interest rates and associated costs when calculating your takeaway, there won't be any surprises. Again, it's just a cost of doing business.

Private lending is best for the quick flip because the shorter the term of borrowing, the less important the interest rate becomes. Keeping a high interest rate for the long term will kill your cash flow, so use private money as an option only when you find a great flipping opportunity.

YOU CAN GET A MORTGAGE

You don't need to make as much money as you think in order to qualify for a non-traditional mortgage. Using private lenders, it's possible to secure a mortgage and still come out ahead.

A high-rate mortgage may be a great option if you want to start investing in real estate, especially if you pay attention to the circumstances. As in any real estate investment, buyers need to be aware of the timing and market fluctuations—and always have an exit strategy.

Timing is the biggest concern if you have a high-rate mortgage, because you don't want to continue to pay too much interest over the long term. The sooner you can get out of the high-rate mortgage, the better, and the more profit you'll realize. If it takes you longer than expected to flip the property, you also run the risk of the market changing. A hot market probably won't change too much in three months, but all bets are off if it takes six months to a year.

Speed is your friend, and time is your enemy. One way to avoid the time drain is to avoid doing the renovations yourself. What might take you six months to finish can be finished by a professional in one to three months. Unless, of course, you hire the wrong contractor! In addition to selling the house sooner, a quick turnaround also saves you the costs associated with holding the property.

Market fluctuations are always a concern if you're flipping a property but can be especially important if you're paying more for your loan. If the market drops, you won't be able to maximize your profit, because you'll have to hang on to it until the market picks up again or sell at a less than desired price. Your project may not be profitable if you're stuck with a higher interest rate for six months instead of three. Try to time the purchase of the property so the renovations are complete at the time of sale, and the time of sale is at the height of the market.

Regardless of where you get financing for your real estate investments, always have a way to exit. Think of your exit strategy as your backup plan. Generally, there are three ways to exit a high-rate mortgage. If the property is a flip, your first plan is usually to sell it as quickly as possible. But what if it's not viable to flip the property? If the market changes while you are completing the renovations, plan B is to treat the property as a "buy and hold." Find out in the beginning of your project what the market looks like for rentals, and run the numbers to make sure renting is a possibility. One other caveat if you are buying into a strata is to make sure renting the property is an allowable option.

A third option as part of your exit strategy is to refinance and get an "A" lender (best available mortgage rate) once you qualify. This may be possible if you now have sweat equity (fruits of your renovations) in the property, your finances have changed, or the renovations make the loan more attractive to a traditional lender. Even if you still don't qualify on your own, you may be able to bring a potential partner into the deal to qualify for a new, lower-interest-rate mortgage.

It's important for your lender to know they are protected, but it's also a good idea to figure out your exit options in the beginning to protect yourself. If you always have a clear plan of action that includes an exit strategy for every project, you will have a much greater chance of success.

WHAT ABOUT MY CREDIT?

Although lending decisions are not based solely on your personal credit score, having good and established credit is always a point in your favour, and it's necessary if applying for a traditional mortgage with an "A" lender. You can easily check your credit score online with Equifax or TransUnion. Lenders generally focus on Equifax over TransUnion in Canada for mortgage lending. Scores range from 300 to 900 and are used by banks to determine credit risk. Currently in Canada, traditional lenders require a minimum score of 620, but there are higher-rate "B" lenders that could still offer a solution for those with credit scores below this level. Want to know where you stand? Go to Equifax.com to obtain your score, and spend the extra money to get the report that comes along with it.

If your score is below 620, you will need a REALLY good story about why your credit has been damaged, or you may need to use "B" lenders that are good for providing mortgages for one to two years to help you re-establish credit and allow you to qualify with an "A" lender in the future. The most difficult mortgage products to qualify for require a 720 Beacon Score, and most lenders require a minimum 650 to 680 score to have access to the best rates available.

There are a number of different factors that can have an effect on your credit score. The most important ones are these:

- Are you paying your credit cards on time? If you are late more than thirty days, your credit score will take a hit. We have seen clients with 800+ Beacon Scores drop to 599 because of two missed payments on a credit card. Often, missing a payment by thirty days can have a huge negative effect on your score.

- How high are the balances that you carry on your credit cards? Once you have established good credit, it is best to pay off the card in full each month. When building credit, however, it can be advantageous to use and carry a balance on the card. Try not to carry a balance over 50 percent of the credit limit each month. If you frequently spend up to $10,000 on your credit card each month, try to obtain a limit of $20,000. Your credit score is substantially affected by your overall credit utilization.

- Do you have any judgments, collections, or bankruptcies on your report? You may have impeccable credit, but a glaring gym membership dispute, for example, can hurt your credit severely. Even cell phone companies now report to the credit bureau, so pay your bills on time!

- How long have you had credit? The longer the credit account has been open and in good standing, the better score you are likely to have.

- What type of credit do you have? It's good to have a mix of credit cards, lines of credit, loans, and so on. Different types of credit will report differently and have different impacts on your score.

Remember that it can take up to six full years for your previous history to be erased. However, even if you have been bankrupt, if you can re-establish a good credit history (two pieces of credit for two years, preferably with a limit of $2,500 or more), it is possible to get a mortgage through an "A" lender.

It is highly recommended that you check your score at least once a year. We always make a point to advise clients of what their score is and how they may be able to improve it. You don't want something as silly as a thirty-dollar unpaid parking ticket to severely affect your credit and cost you thousands in interest.

CHAPTER FIVE

BUILDING THE BAND

When you're just beginning to think about real estate investing, it can be a little overwhelming, even intimidating. The best way to overcome this apprehension is to get education and experience. Another way to get involved quickly at a level of participation that you're comfortable with is to use the power of the group.

In the music business, solo artists often start out as a member of a band as they learn the business. The lead singer may not be able to do it all, and may not want to, so he hires a drummer to keep the beat and musicians to back him up. With every performance as part of the band, he learns more and more that will help him when he's ready to go it alone and reach that rockstar status.

Similarly, having an investment support system that allocates roles can simplify your first projects and allow you to learn and grow with every deal. In the real estate world, who should you include in your investment "band"?

WHO'S ON THE TEAM?

Your deal can have as many partners as you want or as few as two. Regardless of the actual number of participants, there are four main *roles* in every project that must be filled: the deal finder, the cash partner, the qualifying partner, and the managing partner. How you choose to fill the roles will be unique to your project and personal requirements.

First, someone has to find a deal worthy of collaborating on. The role of *deal finder* should be filled by someone who is tied into the market and able to find deals that will make money. The deal finder is often the person who organizes and orchestrates the whole joint venture because they can dig up the deals but may not have the money or be able to get financing.

Finding and negotiating deals that make sense from an investment standpoint can take time. The deal finder needs to have relationships in the industry, while also understanding the sales and rental markets and being able to conduct due diligence on neighbourhoods, schools, employment, crime rates, comparable sales, and so on. A great investment-focused Realtor is another member of the band who can help the deal finder discover and negotiate the best real estate deals. Craigslist, property managers, and investment groups are also good sources of potential properties.

Although it's advisable to use a Realtor when negotiating, you can do it on your own. The best negotiators know the market statistics and understand who has the "upper hand." If properties are flying off the market (seller's market), then there is less negotiating room with the seller. In a buyer's market, however, you may be able to be more creative in your negotiations. For example, you may be able to negotiate long-term closings, vendor take-back mortgages to reduce your down payment, or more favourable terms or prices. If you are negotiating directly with a seller, ask a lot of questions about what they are trying to achieve so you can find unique ways to offer a win-win solution.

The second role in a joint venture is the *cash partner*. Once a good deal is found, you have to have a way to close as soon as possible. If it's a hot deal in a hot market, you have to be able to write an offer immediately. Competition can be stiff, and it's not unusual for people to write offers sight unseen, with no inspections or financing approvals. If you have to wait a week or even a day, the deal could be gone.

If you don't have a credit line or available cash, you should have potential cash partners lined up so that you can move quickly. No need to panic, however. If the deal is really good, you shouldn't have any trouble finding a cash partner eager to get a great return on their investment.

Investors usually get excited by a hot market due to the number of available buyers. Sometimes, however, you'll find the best deals when the market is going down. At these times, there may be fewer buyers, but this just means the sellers aren't getting as many offers and are more motivated. If they need to sell and the offers aren't pouring in, they may be willing to take your under-market bid.

The cash partner is not necessarily the same as the next role in your joint venture, the *qualifying partner*. The cash partner is the person with money for the down payment, renovations, and closing costs, but the qualifying partner is the one who can qualify for the mortgage, loan, or line of credit.

If the cash partner is not the same as the qualifying partner, keep in mind that they must both be attached to the mortgage application. Having both parties on the mortgage is especially important if you are dealing with non-related partners, because you can't gift funds for this purpose outside of immediate family members.

The final role that must be filled in every joint venture is the *managing partner*. The managing partner is the point person who deals with everything related to the property. This partner manages the property or works with a property manager hired for that purpose. They handle the renovations, the tenants, the sale, and so on.

Although you don't necessarily need experience in renovations or contracting to be the managing partner, you have to be willing to do a little babysitting. It's fine to let a general contractor handle the subcontractors, but you need to stay on top of the progress and constantly ask for updates. Every day your renovation takes longer than planned equates to less money in the pockets of the partners.

If you're willing to act as the managing partner, it's not unusual to ask for extra profit in return for handling the project. When you structure your deal, everyone can invest the same amount, but you can charge a management fee of 10 percent for handling the day-to-day work. If the project has a return of $100,000, you take $10,000 off the top and the remaining $90,000 would be split equally among all of the partners (yourself included).

THE JOINT VENTURE

In its simplest form, a joint venture is when multiple parties join together to do one transaction. Often, different partners bring different value to the table. For example, one partner may have cash but need a joint venture partner with experience in construction. On the residential side of financing, a potential investor may be unable to qualify for a mortgage and seek out a partner who can.

The joint venture allows you to get into real estate investing in a structured, partnered way when you are unable to do it on your own. There are no specific ways to set up the joint venture, since it will depend on what is needed for each specific deal. The general idea, however, is to bring in other parties to fill the gaps where you're lacking or where you'd like some help.

We've participated in joint ventures in numerous ways, each one different from the next. You'll discover this for yourself as well because there's no uniform way to structure every deal. You may decide to have four people each contributing 25 percent, or a fifty-fifty deal with just one other partner. We've had situations where we do the research and find the property, negotiate the deal, contribute the down payment, close the deal, and hold the mortgage, then partner with a contractor to fund and complete the renovations.

When you get creative, the joint venture will allow you to do a lot more than you might do on your own. With good joint venture partners, you can work many flips at a time. On your own, you may only be able to handle one in the beginning, maybe two at the most.

Even with all of our experience, we usually prefer joint ventures due to the number of projects we can work on at one time. The upside potential is unlimited once you master the art of working with the right partners.

THE PROS AND CONS OF THE JOINT VENTURE

We've already touched on this a little, but the biggest factor in favour of the joint venture is that it gets you in the deal when there are reasons you can't do it on your own. If you don't have money, can't qualify for a loan, or don't yet have a strong network, joint ventures are a great option.

The joint venture is the solution for the problem of your own lack of experience. The chances of your success in the beginning go way up when you're working from combined experience as opposed to only your own. You'll always find better solutions when more minds are working on a problem.

Having more people involved will also be a help if you want to own numerous properties. Depending on lending rules, it may be difficult to own more than five properties at a time. Even so, you can build a large portfolio if that is your end goal. One of the easiest ways to own multiple properties is to bring in others who are able to be the beneficial owners.

When others are involved, the amount of risk to each individual also goes down. Joint ventures spread the risk and reduce the amount of time and money you might potentially lose on a bad deal.

On the flip side, with risk comes reward. A "con" of the joint venture is that additional partners get a percentage of the profit. The pie has to be cut into more slices once the deal is done. If the profit on a deal is $100,000, you keep it all if you managed it solo. Involve four partners, and your share is only $25,000. You have to weigh the risks versus the rewards in order to find the deal that you're most comfortable with and that has the greatest chance of success.

Another disadvantage of the joint venture is that you lose some control over the project if more people are involved. Depending upon the way the deal is structured, your vote may not be controlling, and the opinions and judgments of others will weigh more heavily. If control over the project is imperative for you, structure your deals accordingly.

Dealing with the decisions or attitudes of others is not

the only complication you will potentially face in a joint venture. Things can, and occasionally will, go wrong. What happens if a partner wants out mid-deal and the renovations aren't complete? What if you aren't able to get the financing to finish the project? Wasn't this joint venture meant to simplify your investment?

PROTECT YOURSELF

Be aware that the complications of life continue to go on even in the midst of your joint venture. Your partner may get injured or become critically ill. They might get divorced or sued. Or maybe they just aren't the rockstar partner you expected them to be.

When you decide to bring in other parties to share their experience (and the work or expense), choose well. There are many unknowns when you start a project. You will save yourself a lot of headaches in the end if you take the time to find appropriate partners in the beginning.

If you don't already have a personal relationship with a potential partner, you may want to share Equifax reports or talk to past partners to find out how they are to work with. Do the research before you sign the agreement, and your deal will go more smoothly.

Even if you conduct the requisite due diligence, issues

with partners will occur. The best way to protect yourself is to have proper legal agreements in place signed by all parties. Put everything in writing, and document the relationship and how issues will be handled. Make sure all parties share their medium- and long-term goals and expectations, and then memorialize them in the contract. Take the opportunity to negotiate potential conflicts up front instead of being forced to accommodate a partner's problems at a time that is much less advantageous.

The cost of having these agreements drafted and reviewed by an attorney may be another disadvantage to the joint venture, but it's one you can't afford to overlook. As mentioned before, the agreement will set up the relationship, but it should also include an escape plan—your exit strategy.

A common way of handling the end of the relationship for whatever reason is the "shotgun clause." If you need to get out of the deal, the shotgun clause assures an equitable resolution for all parties. Essentially, it's a buy/sell provision in which one person is given the right to offer their share of the deal to their partner at a previously specified price. If the partner does not want to buy, they must then sell their own share to the offering partner at the same specified price. This ensures a fair price because neither party knows if the other will buy or sell. Always discuss potential exit strategies with your own attorney to determine what works in your individual circumstances.

Your joint venture agreement will include all of the pertinent legal details, including a shotgun clause or other emergency exit, but it's also important for all of the partners to come to an agreement regarding the intentions of the investment. How long will you hold the property? How many people need to vote on a refinance or a sale? What happens if just one partner wants out?

Consider this scenario. You're working on a flip with another partner when all of a sudden, the market turns. Your partner doesn't care—he wants his money and wants out now. You know you're going to lose money, and you were the managing partner, so all of your time is down the drain as well.

These situations happen all the time, but they can be prevented. Instead of being at the mercy of a partner in a hurry to finish the deal at the most inopportune time, you could have addressed this potentiality in your original agreement. What if you had a backup plan detailing what happens in this situation? For example, your agreement might say that if you don't get a minimum sale amount, then you hold it for a certain period or until the value reaches a certain level.

Try to think of all of the possible contingencies and address them in a way that makes sense for everyone. For example, what happens if a partner dies or becomes critically ill? What if the market turns and you can't sell? Who pays for major repairs, and how will they be repaid? The best way to address such issues is to find a good lawyer who has experience and knows what can go wrong. They've seen the issues, know where the danger zones lie, and know how to mitigate the risks from the very beginning.

FINDING QUALITY JOINT VENTURE PARTNERS

Good partners are everywhere. There are plenty of people ready and willing to join your band of happy investors if the opportunity is a good one. All you have to do is network, network, network!

Networking is the number-one thing you should be doing to increase your odds of finding deals and finding investors. When the time comes, you want to have a group of people to approach who already know you and trust you. Constantly be building relationships and letting people know your intentions regarding real estate investment. Consider getting business cards that say "Real Estate Investor." They are a cheap and easy way to legitimize yourself.

Join investor groups and attend events tailored to people seeking to do the same things you are. Real estate industry events may last for a few days or a few hours, but they often have speakers who will educate you in the field. You may be able to find smaller get-togethers in your area where like-minded people meet to discuss opportunities. Once you start participating, you'll likely be surprised by the number of opportunities there are to connect with the investment community.

As you meet people and start to expand your network, you will also expand your knowledge and joint venture base. Unfortunately, there are some drawbacks. Joining an investor group will probably involve a fee. If not, it's just a meet-up. Meet-ups can be a fun evening but may not be worth your time if you are serious about investing.

Another downside of attending investor events is that the leader may have motives other than just imparting their wisdom. Be wary of speakers pitching deals or looking for partners in deals they have created. Conduct your own due diligence before spending money on programs or deals that seem too good to be true.

Although it's always a good idea to share ideas and learn from as many people as possible, a common interest isn't enough to make a good partner. As you meet people, you should also be vetting them for their potential as a compatible member of a joint venture team.

Do your research before inviting someone to join forces

on your deal, especially if they are out of your normal network. Check their credit score and look at the past six years of their repayment history. Do they have available credit, or are they maxed out? Have they done this before? Were their past deals successful? Ask for a background or credit report and be willing to share yours as well. If they refuse, consider it a bad sign, and look elsewhere.

Overall, it's always easier dealing with people you know. Meet more people so you know more people; then, cultivate those relationships. Put it out on your social media channels that you are interested in flipping properties. Ask your social network for recommendations for books or seminars on flipping or investment. If you get a response, you may have found someone who merits a more in-depth conversation.

HITTING A SOUR NOTE

When a joint venture goes according to plan, it benefits everyone. Unfortunately, things don't always go according to plan. Knowing and preparing for the most common mistakes people make when embarking on a joint venture should help you avoid the pitfalls.

The first pitfall is not coming to terms with other partners regarding individual intentions. This encompasses all of the things discussed above regarding the disadvantages of the joint venture. It's one of the biggest things that can go wrong, but it's easily the most avoidable if you do one thing—put everything in writing. If you memorialize everyone's mutual intentions in the joint venture agreement, there will be no unfortunate surprises.

Another danger occurs when roles are not defined. Each partner must agree to and understand their responsibility on the project. When you have no agreed-upon roles, everyone—and no one—is responsible for everything, and ultimately, very little gets done.

A coordinated effort is key to success. We saw the results of a joint venture gone wrong with a group of college-aged kids who wanted to get into flipping properties. Other than all putting in money, the project had no organization. Their first mistake was trying to do all of the work themselves. The one-month project ended up taking nine months. There were no defined roles or rules, and they all just decided things on the fly. No one knew what anyone else was accomplishing. Even with good intentions, the project was poorly executed. The end result? Lost money and lost friendships.

Another common mistake is not understanding the requirements of financing. Lenders require that qualifying partners have a cash down payment, which generally means that your cash partner and qualifying partner must be the same person. If not, then the cash partner must also be on the mortgage.

An issue can arise if the cash partner doesn't want to be on the mortgage. When you are on a mortgage, there is a record of it, and it will limit your ability to maximize other opportunities, because you may not qualify for other projects.

To navigate this obstacle, the cash partner needs to give the qualifying partner the money for the down payment ninety days (as of when this book was written) in advance of applying for the loan. If the money has been in the qualifying partner's account for more than ninety days, the lender won't question where it originated. Even so, this is a rare scenario, because few investors will want their money in another's account instead of working for them in their own.

IT'S A NUMBERS GAME

One of the best ways to mitigate potential financial issues with your joint venture partners is to create a budgeting template that you can use on every project (www.rockstarrealestateinvesting.com).The template becomes the project budget and includes everything from the sale price and closing costs to a breakdown of the renovation costs that can be added by your contractor.

Keeping this budget as a living document will help you not only stay on budget but also maximize your profits, because you will be able to cut out items that you don't want or that seem extraneous upon review. For example, once you see all of the numbers, you might choose to seed the yard instead of sod, or eliminate the new roof in favour of new windows.

Use the document to give you a very organized breakdown of all of the expenses associated with each of your projects, as well as to encourage your investor circle. When you know your numbers, you can make them work for you.

HARMONY IN THE DEAL

We hope you'll investigate joint ventures as one more way to get into real estate investing. If you don't have cash, can't qualify for a mortgage, or don't feel like you have the experience necessary, it's a good option, because you can make up for your shortfall with someone else's strength.

The main benefit of the joint venture is that it allows you to use the skillsets of others to complement your own weaknesses. There is strength in the group that can be used to your advantage.

Once you have a potential deal for a joint venture, carefully vet your partners. Fill the appropriate roles, and assign responsibilities. Reconcile the intentions of all of the partners in the project, then memorialize them in a joint venture agreement that is drawn up and reviewed by your attorney. When you plan for the known and expected contingencies, your project will be a hit!

CHAPTER SIX

MASTERING THE ART OF THE FLIP

There are many ways to make money in real estate investment, but one of our favourites is the flip. Flipping properties simply means that you are buying a house or property (usually distressed) at a low price, then making repairs and updates (renovations) so you can sell at a substantially higher price and realize a profit. If you can master the art of minimizing your risks, flipping represents a relatively easy way to make money.

FEAR OF THE FLIP

If flipping is such a good opportunity, why don't more people get on board with flipping? It's the intimidation factor or the fear of the unknown. Most people fear what they don't understand, and this fear is multiplied when it involves money. It's time to face the fear!

MITIGATE THE RISKS

House flipping horror stories abound. The investor who sees himself as a handyman and tries to do it all himself usually has disastrous results. The partners who hire a bargain-basement contractor who takes twice as long miss the market and pay way too much in interest. And what if you buy a property only to find out the renovations will cost twice as much as you budgeted for? These things happen, and a contractor who doesn't know what he or she is doing can have a disastrous outcome.

Although poor results are a possibility, they can usually be prevented or mitigated. The first lesson is to always hire proven professionals if you want your flip to be an easy one. Don't try to do it yourself, even if you're handy. You might be your own worst enemy, and it's definitely a waste of your time. Get a good team to handle the renovations, and you'll be done in two to six weeks instead of two to six months or more. With the right team in place, you can sell, get out, and do it again.

Similarly, hire professionals with good reputations who you know will do the job on time, within or below your budget. As you do more deals, you'll learn which contractors are the best at certain jobs and who can be counted on to make your deal profitable. You will also learn who can't.

Occasionally, you may jump on what you think is a hot deal, only to find out the renovations will cost much more than your projected budget. Don't panic. If you find yourself in a place where profits aren't possible, you can always put the property back on the market as is. In the alternative, you can do the renovations and try to break even but treat it as a learning opportunity. Although it's not nearly as exciting as bringing home wheelbarrows full of money, it's not devastating either.

In fact, we've actually made money in exactly this scenario. Jessi once purchased a property during a hot market with the intention to flip. Time was limited, so he took the risk to purchase the property without a thorough contractor review and quote. After the contractor quotes came in, he realized that he'd purchased a lemon and needed to be creative in order to save the deal. He and his team decided to put the property back on the market to see what would happen. The property had already gone up substantially in value, and they sold it for a $80,000 profit. Yes, that was lucky because the market was hot, but it was the hot market that forced them to purchase without the time for contractor quotes.

A resourceful investor can usually find ways to lessen the risk. Don't be afraid of the flip if the deal makes sense in the beginning. It is a rare situation for investors to lose serious money if they understand and appreciate what they're doing and hire a good and reputable contractor.

TIMING IS EVERYTHING

Timing is also an important factor when looking at the risks of flipping. Never calculate profit as if the market is any different than it is right now. In other words, figure out your numbers as if you were going to do the work and sell the property today, as opposed to going into another season that might "guarantee" more money. If the market goes up, awesome. Consider yourself lucky. Don't roll the dice, however, because there are no guarantees. If the market swings in your favour and you make more money than expected, it's a nice bonus, but don't rely on it. The deal needs to make sense at the time you make it happen.

Even though you can't know exactly what the market will do, you should try to time your projects so that you hit the best buying months. Generally, the best times to buy are in the winter (December and January) and summer (July and August), because the strongest sales occur in spring and fall (primarily spring). Real estate is not always consistent, but we try to pick up the most deals during these times.

The general rule of thumb is that April, May, or June and mid-September are good times to get your renovated properties back on the market. In the late summer, nobody wants to think about a move when they are getting the kids ready to go back to school. It's better to wait until business gets back to normal.

There's also another side to this theory. Smart sellers don't sell during summer and winter months. They won't even list. Inventory may be reduced, but the people who are selling are very motivated (or don't really know what they're doing). All the better for the smart investor!

YOUR FLIPPING TEAM

Before you start looking for your first house to flip, prepare yourself. Line up the experts you will need at each stage of the process. Your team may make the difference in whether your flip is a flop or a profitable real estate investment. The goal is to build a team that will last and that includes a mortgage broker, a real estate agent, a contractor, and a stager.

In order to build a team that you can use repeatedly on similar projects, do the research up front. Consult your network, and solicit word-of-mouth recommendations. Joining a local real estate investing meet-up or club is a good way to meet others and learn from their mistakes and successes. Never take advice or guidance from someone who hasn't experienced the situation first hand. Finally, use Facebook and Google to vet potential team members and read first-hand reviews of their work.

THE MORTGAGE BROKER

The first professional you will be working with is the mortgage broker, in order to get pre-approval for your mortgage. Talk to several, and make sure they have solid recommendations and you feel comfortable working with them. They should be asking you lots of questions, but remember that you are essentially interviewing *them*. You may be working with the same mortgage broker for quite some time, and you will enjoy it much more if you like them and enjoy the way they approach business.

The reason for working with a mortgage broker in the very beginning is that you want to have confidence that when you make an offer, it will be approved. Every broker works differently, but the ideal broker will thoroughly review your documents, explain your options, and give you a pre-approval you can rely on.

If there are many offers for a property, a proper pre-approval may sway the seller in your direction. Your broker can provide a pre-approval letter as proof of financing to show the seller. When competition is stiff, sellers like to know you aren't going to tie up their property for a week or two, then back out due to lack of financing.

THE REALTOR

Instead of scouting the classifieds, you should work with a real estate professional (Realtor) to find opportunities for flipping. Like everyone else on your team, it pays to take the time in the beginning to find a real estate agent who understands investment properties.

Very few real estate agents know how to deal with investors and vet properties for flipping opportunities. Most don't, so don't take them at their word. Instead, ask the important questions and let them prove their expertise. If an agent says they specialize in investment properties, ask them what that means. How do they define what they do as a specialist in real estate investment? What do they consider to be the most important factors that define a good investment opportunity? How many investment transactions have they closed? For more questions to ask potential agents, see our website at www.rockstarrealestateinvesting.com.

Your real estate agent must be very familiar with the market and be able to discuss every potential property. It's not enough simply to have Multiple Listing Service (MLS) access. Make sure your agent can discuss house quality, property quality, potential strata corporation stability, and any related issues, such as rental potential, pet policies, neighbourhoods, and schools.

The "quality of the house" relates to the condition of the house as well as its overall "bones." In addition to the actual house, the "quality of the land" often becomes paramount to the success of a deal. More than just general location, property questions involve characteristics of the lot such as size (i.e., sloping, irregular, unusual characteristics) and if there is anything inherent in the property that might affect resale (i.e., small yard or too close to power lines).

Agents should also be able to provide strata information. Similar to homeowners' associations in the United States, some strata companies will restrict the number of rentals per building, or they may have other arbitrary rules regarding pets or age restrictions. Consider all of the rules and regulations related to the property, because they will affect your ability to resell or may negatively impact your "Plan B" of renting the property if flipping doesn't work out in your favour.

If your agent is well-versed in the area and the state of the market, they should be able to identify the best opportunities for flipping. The perfect house for a flip is usually the most run-down house on a nice street. Generally, you don't want to be the nicest house in a bad neighbourhood. Instead, look to upgrade a poor house in a good neighbourhood to the level of average or slightly above average. If it has holes in the walls and smells of cat urine but is in a good area, you've got a contender!

A good agent should also have a great network and be able to hire or recommend professional stagers, photographers, surveyors, attorneys, and so on. When it comes to marketing your property, the skill of your photographer or videographer is very important. You want a photographer who knows how to light a room to make it look big and bright, and who is able to edit your photographs to show your property at its very best. Twilight shots are also highly recommended. Potential buyers make snap judgments from your pictures. If they're bad, you'll never get the opportunity to show them any differently, because you'll never get the call.

THE CONTRACTOR

The quality and efficiency of a contractor's work affects everything about your project. Your flip is only as good as its renovation, and your profit hinges on your ability to turn the property as quickly as possible.

The quality of contractors varies greatly, so it's not enough simply to pick one and assume you'll get what you pay for.

When you first get started, you'll likely find that bids will be all over the map. The same project might receive a bid of $25,000 from one contractor, and another contractor may say they can do it for $50,000. Who do you trust? The term "you get what you pay for" may be true, but you also have to know your target market. A luxury property requires a much different contractor than a small forty-year-old condo upgrade in the suburbs.

We have learned the hard way how a contractor with the lowest quote may end up costing much more by completion. One of our projects cost almost four times the initial quote (after taking into account the related interest charges) because the contractor took a year to complete what should have been completed in six to eight weeks. We missed the market and had to sell the property at a price about 15 percent lower than we should have. Although we researched the contractor thoroughly, we later found out that he lied about everything. He had zero idea what he was doing. It was a tough lesson to learn.

The key is getting recommendations from people who have firsthand experience working with your potential hire. Call your network and ask around. Go on social media and ask your contacts if they know contractors who work quickly and do quality work at a fair price. Narrow down the recommendations by reliability and price, and only take recommendations from friends who have actually used the candidate and have direct experience with them.

Once you narrow down potential contractors, interview the ones you like best. Ask them about past projects and how active they are in the process. Do they have any current projects where you can take a peek at their work quality? Make sure it's their full-time business, and find out the size of their operation and staff.

Before you ask a contractor to bid on your job, pitch yourself to them. If it's your intention to become an active flipper, let the contractor know you want to build a smooth operating machine that can get projects done in the most efficient way. The opportunity for additional work may be enough of an incentive for the contractor to give you the best quote possible.

We each have contractors whom we routinely use. They work extra hard and provide excellent service because they know we do lots of deals and can be a gold mine for them if they do a great job.

The process of finding good contractors can be time consuming, but it's well worth it once you find ones who work well for your business. Once you get a good quote or find a contractor you like, start them off small and test them out. Consider their first project as a trial. If they do well, move them up to bigger and bigger projects.

THE STAGER

Home staging is the process of preparing a house for a quick sale in the shortest amount of time. We usually think of stagers as coming in at the end of a renovation and doing things to make a house more desirable for buyers, such as rearranging furniture, clearing clutter, or making the space more neutral by getting rid of personal items. Since most buyers decide within the first thirty seconds of looking at a house whether or not it's right for them, using a stager at this point can maximize your impact.

Good home stagers can also be utilized after you buy the house and before the sale to help you create a *plan* for renovations. Consider using a stager when you are investigating the property prior to making an offer. A good stager will have their finger on the pulse of what is trendy and know how to make your property appeal to buyers in the moment.

Have your stager give you a rough idea of what needs to be done to make the house the most marketable for the least cost. You can give the stager's recommendations to your contractor to get the maximum results from the cost of your renovation.

We offer a flat fee to our stagers for the initial assessment—usually $250 to $500 depending on the requirement of their time. With the assessment, we ask for the design elements as well. Designers can be very expensive ($7,000 to $12,000 for just a condo), but a stager can give you the kind of design advice you need (paint colours, flooring, light fixtures, etc.) for a fraction of the cost.

RENOVATING YOUR PROPERTY

Your stager will provide you with the ideas you need to make renovation decisions. Neutrality is key. Your goal is to make the house appeal to the greatest number of people in order to increase the odds of a fast sale and hopefully get competing offers. One offer will get you a sale, but two competing offers will get you the most profit, because you can play them off of each other.

If your real estate agent did their job successfully, you got a great deal on a house that needed enough work so that no one else wanted it, but not so much work that renovations aren't feasible. As discussed previously, the structure of the house and the major systems should be intact and fully operational.

Try to avoid making any structural changes to the house or changes that require permits. Making such substantial changes can eat up your time and money and lower the return on your investment. Once you start changing the foundation or tearing out walls, you may find that the wiring is bad or the plumbing isn't up to par. Your costs will skyrocket on things that are unseen by the consumer—things they don't want to pay for.

Instead, focus on the "lipstick."

The "lipstick" changes that we recommend are the little things that aren't too expensive but make a huge difference in terms of buyer opinion (and ROI). Concentrate your efforts on the things that bring maximum results, meaning maximum revenue, at a minimum cost.

The most basic and bare-bones "lipstick" renovation includes things like flooring, paint, kitchen, and bathrooms. Even smaller things like lighting fixtures, lighting switches, landscaping, and power washing the driveway will make a big difference. It's getting easier to add the "wow" factor to flips, because home-improvement stores have gotten very savvy about copying and offering the most expensive styles for less.

Start with a reasonable plan for renovations, and implement it in a cost-effective way. Have a plan so you don't get so caught up in the excitement of making the flip fabulous that you price yourself out of the market.

Before and after photos of one of Jessi's flips. Notice how the upgrades aren't miraculous, but are functional and would be above average (generally not high-end). The upgrades usually focus on brightening the unit and opening the space.

You were smart to buy the worst house on the nicest street in a good area. Your goal now is to upgrade it to being an average (or slightly above average) house on a nice street. Your goal is not to create the *nicest* house in the neighbourhood. The reasoning is that buyers will not want to pay for what they view as the mansion on a crappy street. Know your market and stay in your lane. When you stay middle-of-the-road, the comparables will work to your benefit.

FLIPPING IN A NUTSHELL

Once you complete your mortgage pre-approval, let your Realtor know that you are interested in a new investment so they can gather a portfolio of potential flips that match your criteria. Conduct your own due diligence, do your own research, and look at the data. Once your decision is made, your Realtor will work to obtain the property for you through writing offer(s).

Then, bring in your stager. For $250 (sometimes $500 depending on the time requirement), the stager walks around the interior and exterior of the house and lists everything they think you need to do (or re-do) to take the house to the most marketable condition for the least cost, while appealing to the greatest number of buyers. This list will include things like grout colour, fixtures, hardware, paint colour codes, flooring specifics, and so on. After determining your budget, hand the list off to a few contractors (unless you have someone already decided on) to provide quotes.

The entire process takes approximately three months (one month to line everything up and then another month or two for the renovations). Once renovations are complete, bring the stager back for final staging. The Realtor then brings in their professional photographer to take amazing pictures and videos. Ideally, you want to be ready for sale at peak market time. We recommend that you slightly underprice the property to provoke a "feeding frenzy" of offers. Cha-ching!

KEEPING TRACK

Although we've said it before, it bears repeating: real estate investment is a numbers game. Get the numbers right and you win, get them wrong and you stand to lose quite a bit. The tricky part is keeping up with all the moving parts of your ongoing project, particularly when unknowns pop up and things change.

The flip analysis is a tool (see our website at www.rock-starrealestateinvesting.com) that you can use to make sure you don't forget any of your expenses. With the flip analysis, you can calculate a break-even point so you know how long you can hold the property and still realize a profit. Once you input your purchase price, expected renovation costs, expected sale price, timelines for renovation and sale, and your holding costs, you should be able to calculate the return on your investment and determine if it's a rockstar flip or one that's not worth your time.

Beginning investors often forget about costs such as Realtor fees, taxes, legal fees, and lender fees. Using the analysis will help you keep a close eye on the expenses and accurately calculate entry and exit costs to ensure your project is a good deal. Also, remember that you'll have to set aside money from your profit to pay capital-gains taxes. Since taxes are always subject to change, remember to seek guidance from an accredited accountant who can keep you informed.

When running your numbers, always look at the worst-case scenario. The market can turn quickly. What will happen if it's not a good time to sell? Can you still hold onto it and recoup cash flow using it as a rental? Before you buy a property, figure out what happens if your golden deal turns into a "buy and hold."

Believe what the numbers tell you. Avoid the emotional attachment to properties you love, and focus solely on your bottom line. If you know your numbers and they show you the deal won't be as profitable as you need it to be, walk away. There's always another, better deal waiting for you when you're a rockstar.

FLIPPING FORWARD

Flipping properties as a real estate investment strategy is not out of reach for the beginner investor, particularly if you educate yourself on the process. The worst-case scenario is that you will have to refinance up to 80 percent and hold it until the tide turns.

Let's assume you are buying a property to flip that is currently valued at $500,000. You put down a $100,000 down payment, secure a $400,000 mortgage, and put $50,000 into renovations. You've spent $150,000, but when it's done, the property should appraise for over $650,000. You can go back to the bank and refinance up to 80 percent of the new value, which equates to $520,000. Now, you can get $120,000 back out of the home equity, which means you just bought a $650,000 home for roughly $30,000, plus closing costs. Bravo!

Now, let's assume that you get a really good deal when buying the home and the market is on an upswing. This same property could easily be worth $700,000 or more, and when you refinance that up to 80 percent of the value, you can now mortgage the property to $560,000, which means that you essentially were just "paid" $10,000 to buy this property! Minus closing costs, of course. Now that is a sweet deal!

Even if the market stalls and you can't sell quickly, the "buy and hold" strategy can be very lucrative because your renters are growing your equity for you every month. The only wild card in this scenario is the new appraised value. Minimize this risk by always being conservative in your calculations.

Another great way to minimize your risks flipping prop-erty is to assemble a hard-working, trustworthy team. With a knowledgeable and professional mortgage broker and real estate agent, you will be able to find and buy the best properties. With efficient and qualified stagers and contractors, you will be able to accomplish cost-effective and beautiful renovations in a timely way. With a great team to support you, you will realize your goals of making money flipping properties. So, what are you waiting for? Get to work!

ANATOMY OF A FLIP

PURCHASE

Purchase price:	$600,000.00
Closing costs:	$10,914.43
Legal fees:	$1,211.16
Renovation:	$89,451.55
Operating costs:	$4,754.79
Total:	**$706,331.93**

SALE

Sale price:	$790,000.00
Staging:	$4,246.40
Closing costs:	$1,168.21
Profit:	**$78,253.46**

Total time from purchase to sale: less than three months.

CHAPTER SEVEN

BUYING A $1 CONDO

If you've made it this far into the book, you're probably starting to realize that real estate investing is one of the safest and easiest ways to increase your bottom line and build wealth for the future. If so, congratulations! You are well on your way to transforming your new knowledge into a better financial outlook.

So, what's the best way to get started? One of the most exciting deals to try if you want to get your feet wet is the "$1 condo." Sometimes, you may pay nothing for a condo or even get paid to buy it at the end of the day! Although you can use the same strategy with a house, starting with a condo makes sense because the risk is not as great. Start small to build your confidence and learn as you go.

The concept of the $1 condo is that you buy a property for 20 percent down and do the renovations needed to get it up in value. Then you refinance, pull your money out, and rent the property for positive cash flow. It's just that easy if you know what you are doing.

There have been multiple times we have literally been paid to acquire a property. If you get the numbers right, you can get more out of the refinance than you put down, and the property pays for itself with the rental income. In the meantime, you're still building equity in the property, and you have no cash tied up in it whatsoever. Let's look at the details.

CASHING IN ON THE REFINANCE

The key to making this strategy work is being hyper-vigilant in making sure you buy in the right area for the right price. The property and the timing of the deal are the most important considerations. Take your time in the beginning, and shop around until you find a run-down condo (for example) in a building and area that are still desirable. To get the best deal, make sure you are purchasing in winter or summer so your lowball offer (ideally) makes sense to the owner.

Using the previous chapter as a guide, follow the tips and techniques for flipping. Count on spending at least

$5,000 to $25,000 for the renovations for a lower-end condo. Remember that you aren't trying to change floor plans or make major structural changes. Focus on the "lipstick"—the superficial changes that make a big difference in the marketability of your property and, most importantly, in the eyes of the buyer.

Once your renovation is complete, get a new appraisal through your mortgage broker or bank. The new appraisal will be used to refinance your property with a mortgage. Most lenders will refinance up to 80 percent of the new value. If your numbers were right in the beginning, you'll be able to redeem the purchase price of the property, and voilà: the $1 condo (or maybe even better)!

Be aware that some lenders may require that you hold the property for a certain amount of time before refinancing. Find out a lender's policy before you buy, and simply avoid the ones that won't let you take advantage of this strategy. Although it's something to consider and investigate in the beginning, most lenders will let you refinance, or "top up," once you've renovated the property.

The strategy of buying, renovating, and refinancing can be used in many scenarios. Use it to meet your original goals, or use the "refinance and rent" strategy as discussed in the last chapter. Turning your sale property into a rental is a great tactic if you get stuck with a property if the market turns, and refinancing will put the money back in your pocket immediately.

As always, pick the strategy that matches your intentions. Are you trying to build a collection of ten properties to rent while building equity? This strategy can keep your cash liquid and available for reinvestment as you constantly renovate and refinance. Or is it your intention to get quick cash? Instead of building a book of ten properties, use this strategy to renovate and flip a property every two to three months. Please keep in mind that, in Canada, it's very hard to qualify for mortgages to buy more properties, and most lenders do not allow you to purchase or own more than five doors (five properties).

$1 CONDO CASE STUDY

The $1 condo refers to a technique where you refinance up to the amount it costs to complete the purchase and renovation as shown below. Essentially, we bought a condo for $1 that still has $36,625 in equity!

PURCHASE

Purchase price:	$64,000.00
Closing costs:	$1,736.40
Legal fees:	$1,078.67
Renovation:	$21,560.00
Total:	**$88,375.07**

REFINANCE

Appraised value:	$125,000.00
Refinance at 70.7%:	**$88,375.00**

IT'S A TEAM EFFORT

Regardless of your intention, you need to have a team in place that can help you reach your goals. As with joint ventures and traditional flips, the first thing you need to do is put a great team together. A mortgage broker can help you determine the best way to finance the deal and find lenders that don't have negative rules regarding refinancing.

When looking for your own $1 condo project, your Realtor is the most important member of your team, because everything hinges on finding the right property. When you do enough of these deals, your Realtor will already know what you're looking for and what is required to make your deal work.

Work closely with your real estate agent to make sure your questions are answered. For example, is the condo in a building without issues? What is the condition of the shared space? How strong is the contingency fund? Is the boiler in good repair? Is the roof in good shape? Are there any upcoming assessments? Other questions might relate to the status of the building management and anything that might affect future costs. For example, have there been constant special assessments? How are the strata's financials? Are there water ingress issues?

Remember that unexpected issues do occur. In order

to err on the side of caution, we recommend a contingency fund of $2,500 to $3,500 per unit to deal with these unforeseen or unpredictable matters. It's always better to be prepared and not have a problem than for something to pop up that you are not prepared to deal with.

Finally, you need to have a good idea about the rental conditions in the area and especially in the building that you are considering buying! You never know if you will need to rent out the property, so don't buy into a building that bans or restricts rentals. Are there any conditions or building rules regarding how long you are allowed to rent the condo? What would the rental rate be at current conditions? What is the expected rental rate after the renovations? Make sure your real estate agent has not only the ability to find properties but also the expertise to help you assess their potential. A good website to help you quickly learn about market rents in a particular area is Rentometer.com.

If you follow the team-building guidelines previously discussed, you will bring a stager with you to help determine the scope and details of the renovations. The stager's notes will help the contractor give you an estimate of costs. With a lower-price property like a condo, you may realize only 20 percent in profits, for example. While still a great profit margin, you start losing money very quickly if your contractor goes over budget or takes too long to finish the job. Being aware of this pitfall is the best way to prevent it. Stay involved in the process and on top of the progress so you can put a halt to problems before they blow up and cost you money.

THE POWER OF A DOLLAR

Condos are a great place to start your journey as a real estate investor. The stakes are lower, and the projects are more manageable. If you start at the price level of a condo, you will gradually build credibility with lenders, which will help you as you grow into bigger and more lucrative properties.

When deals are smaller, the profit potential is often smaller as well, so you have to be vigilant. Make sure you pick the right property and pay close attention to your numbers. The upside is that if you do make mistakes, the potential for loss is much smaller as well.

Use the strategy outlined in this chapter to get out there and explore your potential as an investor. There's no harm in doing deals in the beginning where you make little to no money, as long as you're learning. Even Gene Simmons had to start somewhere, and it wasn't on stage in front of millions!

In the beginning, you may even want to consider finding a money partner and contributing the time and work yourself, even if you agree to forego a share of the profits. Think of it as an "investment internship." You get to learn the business from an expert, with no risk to your bank account!

If you aren't making mistakes, you aren't trying hard enough. Luckily, you don't have to do it alone. Use this book, our website at www.rockstarrealestateinvesting. com, your own real estate team, and the investment community in your area to learn as you go. You'll be comfortably rocking solo in no time!

CHAPTER EIGHT

NEXT-LEVEL INVESTING

Once you've mastered the basics of finding money to invest, combining forces through a joint venture, building a team, and flipping or renting properties, you may be ready to add a few more instruments to your investment band. If you're feeling especially bold, consider the following advanced strategies that can give you additional moneymaking opportunities.

RENT-TO-OWN

Offering your tenants the opportunity to rent-to-own (RTO) the property they're living in is a lucrative strategy if you don't mind holding the property for a while. In the rent-to-own scenario, an investor buys a property on behalf of a person (tenant) who cannot qualify for the loan or doesn't have the down payment. The tenant then agrees to purchase the property from the investor/landlord at a set price in the future. In theory, the investor might also rent to a tenant without the stated income, but it's better to stick to tenants who lack either the credit or funds to purchase immediately.

The RTO makes sense for the investor because they can set a feasible exit strategy and clearly map out the return on their investment. Market appreciation is already included in the contract because the tenant agrees to pay a set market price by a certain date. As in any lease, rent is set according to market standards. Above the normal rent, however, the tenant pays an additional amount, which builds up his deposit and eventually becomes the down payment for purchase. Everything is planned out from day one to make sure the tenant will qualify to buy the property in the specified timeframe.

One potential roadblock to the purchase may occur if the market doesn't appreciate as expected. For example, the purchase price may be set at the current value plus 10 percent appreciation per year, equating to $350,000. Over the course of the tenancy, the appreciation falls and there is a significant difference in the market value. Then, the property is only worth $300,000 at the contracted time of purchase. What happens now?

The way this situation is handled depends upon how you structure your rent-to-own contract. Sometimes, the tenancy will continue until the property reaches the value as originally contemplated (at no additional cost to the tenant). The alternative is that you may decide the price remains at the price agreed upon regardless of market variations.

If your contract requires that the price stay the same even if the property hasn't appreciated as expected, there is an additional complication. If the purchase price remains higher than the current value, a bank will only lend the tenant the amount of the appraised value minus the down payment. In order to abide by the contract, the tenant may have to come up with the additional $50,000, which may be difficult if not impossible. Keep this in mind when you enter into the deal, and cover all of the contingencies up front.

Rent-to-own deals are full of advantages for both parties. The tenant is given the opportunity to buy a house that they otherwise would be unable to buy. While helping a potential homeowner has a wonderful "feel good" quality to it for the investor, there are other benefits as well.

As already discussed, the investor benefits from knowing they will recoup a pre-set price on the home as well as getting monthly rent to pay the expenses. The overall down payment for the investor decreases, while the overall return increases. In addition, the investor has a tenant who will probably take great care of the property because they have a vested interest.

Regardless of what happens at the end of the tenancy, the investor wins. If everything goes according to plan, the tenant buys the property at the end of the predetermined time at the predetermined price. A happy ending!

Sometimes, however, the tenant decides they don't want the house or can't go through with the transaction for whatever reason. Perhaps they're moving or lost their job, or perhaps they weren't able to improve their credit. If the tenant walks away, you keep the rent and the extra money that has accumulated for the down payment. We had a tenant walk away from an RTO deal after putting $68,000 into it. It happens. You can then flip the property or find another tenant. Still a happy ending!

THE MULTIPLIER EFFECT

The multiplier effect comes into play if you are investing in multi-family or commercial properties. In Canada, lenders consider anything over five residential units to come under the spectrum of commercial financing.

The strategy of using the multiplier effect is generally

applied to apartment buildings, and the best way to understand it is to understand the capitalization, or cap, rate. The cap rate is the rate of return on your commercial real estate investment based on the income it is expected to generate. If you know your net operating expenses (revenue from the property minus all reasonable, necessary operating expenses) and the current market value, you can determine the cap rate of a given property. The cap rate is equal to the net operating income divided by the current market value.

For example, if you own a building that is worth $1 million and has a net operating income of $100,000, the cap rate is 10 percent. The percentage rate identifies the rate of return an investor would expect to receive if they were to buy that building with cash (no mortgage) and is an indicator of what someone is willing to pay in a certain marketplace. It's important to note that financing costs and extraneous costs like renovations and maintenance are not included in this calculation. Only expenses expected to continue on an ongoing basis should be factored in.

Knowing the cap rate makes it easier to understand the magic of the multiplier effect. If you can improve your net operating income, you improve the value of your property. If the net operating income increases by $10,000 in the above example, you've actually improved the value of the building by $100,000. In other words, someone would be willing to pay an additional $100,000 to receive $10,000 per year back in revenue in that market.

MULTIPLIER EFFECT CASE STUDY

A great example of the multiplier effect in its simplest form is proven by an investment group that became one of the largest multi-family owners in Phoenix, Arizona, in only a few years. They had an apartment building with two hundred units tied up under contract. One of the beautiful things about this property was that the closets in the units actually had hook-ups for washers and dryers, but none were installed. They slipped a notice under each of the doors asking if the tenants would pay an additional fifty dollars per month to have a washer and dryer installed. About one hundred units, half of the building, opted in. With this increase of $600 per unit per year, the Net Operating Income (NOI) of the building increased by $60,000. In Phoenix, the cap rate is about 6 percent, which means that installing the washers and dryers increased the value of the building by $1 million. The cost of installation? Only about $1,500 per unit! Plus, they were able to refinance the building a year later and pull out 75 percent of the increase in value, so they put in about $150,000 and were able to pull $750,000 in cash right back out of the building, generating $600,000 in cash right out of thin air!

The investment group likes to joke that they aren't in the real estate business—they're in the washer and dryer business. The lesson is that the idea doesn't have to be complicated. Often, the idea can be very simple—it's the magic of the multiplier!

We are considering writing another book focusing on the multiplier effect, because it really is a unique way of building wealth.

THE VENDOR TAKE-BACK

The vendor take-back is another financing option in which the seller gives the buyer the mortgage necessary to buy their property. Instead of the bank holding your loan, the owner of the property acts as your lender. The owner might also offer financing in addition to what a bank offers in order to make a deal work.

The vendor take-back works for owners who want to sell but also want cash flow on an ongoing basis. An additional benefit for the seller/lender is that there is potential in Canada to defer capital gains for up to five years in this scenario.

The owner may choose to fund the entire mortgage or just a portion. From the buyer's standpoint, borrowing from the owner is a way to simplify the lending process. If available, the buyer can use the vendor take-back option for the whole mortgage or to make up the difference if a bank isn't willing to lend the entire purchase price. For example, if a bank is willing to lend 80 percent of the purchase price, you might get 10 percent from the seller and only have to come up with a 10 percent down payment.

THE TAKE-BACK SAVES THE DEAL

On Kyle's first joint venture, the lender bailed for no apparent reason. Luckily, he was able to figure out alternative financing and close the deal.

On the day we were supposed to fund the transaction, my business partner made the three-hour drive to the credit union, only to find out it had decided to back out of the deal. I have yet to find out why!

Although I had a backup plan from another lender, it wasn't enough. The new lender was willing to fund the deal very quickly, but they wouldn't give us quite enough to make the deal work. My partner and I could make a down payment but decided to approach the sellers to make up the shortfall.

Although the real estate agents were completely against the idea, I met with the seller directly and explained what had happened. I told him that we still wanted to complete the deal but would need a vendor take-back of $160,000. It saved the deal, and the seller even gave us a 6 percent interest-only loan, instead of the 7 percent I initially offered.

The key to this deal was that the property had very good cash flow, so borrowing the extra money at a higher interest rate didn't affect our bottom line.

CONCLUSION

THE BIG FINISH

Q: How do you get to Carnegie Hall?

A: Practice, practice, practice!

Many of the biggest rockstars in the world have played at Carnegie Hall, but they didn't get there overnight. Their journey started with a few basic steps—picking up an instrument, practicing a riff, overcoming their fears—and then doing them over and over again in order to learn their craft.

The same thing applies to you and your new career as a real estate investor. Congratulations on picking up this book and educating yourself—you are well on your way!

You've taken the best step forward, but you can't stop now. Jump in and start with a small deal so you can learn by doing, practice your new skills, and master *your* craft.

Start by setting your intentions and goals moving forward. Do you want to make quick cash by flipping, or would you rather create steady cash flow through buying and holding? Are you ready to go it alone, or do you want a partner?

Need help finding a partner or group to join? Reach out to us. We are creating a flipping community for people to meet potential partners. First, we just have to figure out what you bring to the table and where you would fit in "the band." Sometimes we also allow people to buy into flips—just ask!

Figure out your financial strengths and weaknesses, and know where you might need help. Create a game plan. Find a partner for a joint venture, or combine forces with someone who's been in the business for a while and can teach you as you work through your first deals.

Most importantly, don't be a victim of "analysis paralysis" or get too intimidated to move forward on your own path to creating wealth. You should definitely continue to read books or take classes and constantly be learning more about real estate investment, but don't let fear of the unknown get in the way of your future. For helpful tools, tips, and a little motivation, check out www.rock-starrealestateinvesting.com.

You picked up this book because you knew you could be a rockstar in the world of real estate. We know you can, too. It's possible, and the deals are out there waiting for you to bring your new skills and expertise. There is no time better than the present to get started!

Much love, Jessi & Kyle

GLOSSARY

Amenity: A feature of the home or property that serves as a benefit to the buyer but that is not necessary to its use; may be natural (like location, woods, water) or man-made (like a swimming pool or garden).

Amortization: Repayment of a mortgage loan through monthly installments of principal and interest; the monthly payment amount is based on a schedule that will allow you to own your home at the end of a specific time period (for example, fifteen or thirty years).

Annual Percentage Rate (APR): Calculated by using a standard formula, the APR shows the cost of a loan; expressed as a yearly interest rate, it includes the interest, points, mortgage insurance, and other fees associated with the loan.

Application: The first step in the official loan approval process; this form is used to record important information about the potential borrower necessary to the underwriting process.

Appraisal: A document that gives an estimate of a property's fair market value; an appraisal is generally required by a lender before loan approval to ensure that the mortgage loan amount is not more than the value of the property.

Appraiser: A qualified individual who uses his or her experience and knowledge to prepare the appraisal estimate.

ARM: Adjustable Rate Mortgage; a mortgage loan subject to change in interest rates; when rates change, ARM monthly payments increase or decrease at intervals determined by the lender; the change in monthly payment amount, however, is usually subject to a cap.

Assumable Mortgage: A mortgage that can be transferred from a seller to a buyer; once the loan is assumed by the buyer, the seller is no longer responsible for repaying it; there may be a fee and/or a credit package involved in the transfer of an assumable mortgage.

Borrower: A person who has been approved to receive a loan and is then obligated to repay it and any additional fees according to the loan terms.

Budget: A detailed record of all income earned and spent during a specific period of time.

Building Code: Based on agreed-upon safety standards within a specific area, a building code is a regulation that determines the design, construction, and materials used in building.

Cap: A limit, such as that placed on an adjustable rate mortgage, on how much a monthly payment or interest rate can increase or decrease.

Cash Reserves: A cash amount sometimes required to be held in reserve in addition to the down payment and closing costs; the amount is determined by the lender.

Certificate of Title: A document provided by a qualified source (such as a title company) that shows the property legally belongs to the current owner; before the title is transferred at closing, it should be free and clear of all liens or other claims.

Closing: Also known as settlement, this is the time at which the property is formally sold and transferred from the seller to the buyer; it is at this time that the borrower takes on the loan obligation, pays all closing costs, and receives the title from the seller.

Closing Costs: Customary costs above and beyond the sale price of the property that must be paid to cover the transfer of ownership at closing; these costs generally vary by geographic location and are typically detailed to the borrower after submission of a loan application.

CMHC: Canada Mortgage and Housing Corporation is run by the Canadian government. This entity insures mortgages anytime a client puts less than 20 percent down on a purchase, which protects the bank from losses if the client defaults. This is a cost to the borrower, but there is no benefit for the borrower. Do not confuse this form of insurance with home insurance or life insurance.

Commission: An amount, usually a percentage of the property sales price, that is collected by a real estate professional as a fee for negotiating the transaction.

Condominium: A form of ownership in which individuals purchase and own a unit of housing in a multi-unit complex; the owner also shares financial responsibility for common areas.

Conventional Loan: A private-sector loan, one that is not guaranteed or insured by a mortgage insurer like CMHC or Genworth.

Credit Bureau Score: A number representing the possibility a borrower may default; it is based upon credit history and is used to determine ability to qualify for a mortgage loan.

Credit History: History of an individual's debt payment; lenders use this information to gauge a potential borrower's ability to repay a loan.

Debt Servicing Ratio: A comparison of gross income to housing and non-housing expenses. Typically, lenders want the monthly mortgage payment and other housing debts not to exceed 32 percent of monthly gross income (before taxes), and the mortgage payment combined with non-housing debts should not exceed 40 percent of income.

Default: The inability to pay monthly mortgage payments in a timely manner or to otherwise meet the mortgage terms.

Delinquency: Failure of a borrower to make timely mortgage payments under a loan agreement.

Down Payment: The portion of a home's purchase price that is paid in cash and is not part of the mortgage loan.

Equity: An owner's financial interest in a property; calculated by subtracting the amount still owed on the mortgage loan(s) from the fair market value of the property.

Fair Market Value: The hypothetical price that a willing buyer and seller will agree upon when they are acting freely, carefully, and with complete knowledge of the situation.

Fixed-Rate Mortgage: A mortgage with payments that remain the same throughout the life of the loan because the interest rate and other terms are fixed and do not change.

Foreclosure: A legal process in which mortgaged property is sold to pay the loan of the defaulting borrower.

Home Inspection: An examination of the structure and mechanical systems to determine a home's safety; makes the potential homebuyer aware of any repairs that may be needed.

Homeowner's Insurance: An insurance policy that combines protection against damage to a dwelling and its contents with protection against claims of negligence or inappropriate action that results in someone's injury or property damage.

Insurance: Protection against a specific loss over a

period of time that is secured by the payment of a regularly scheduled premium.

Interest: A fee charged for the use of money; the time value of money.

Interest Rate: The amount of interest charged on a monthly loan payment; usually expressed as a percentage.

Lien: A legal claim against property that must be satisfied when the property is sold.

Loan: Money borrowed that is usually repaid with interest.

Loan Fraud: Purposely giving incorrect information on a loan application in order to better qualify for a loan; may result in civil liability or criminal penalties.

Loan-to-Value (LTV) Ratio: A percentage calculated by dividing the amount borrowed by the price or appraised value of the home to be purchased; the higher the LTV, the less cash a borrower is required to pay as down payment.

Lock-In: Since interest rates can change frequently, many lenders offer an interest rate lock-in that allows clients in a variable rate to lock in to a fixed rate. When dealing with branch banks, beware that they often will not guarantee their best rates when you lock in, so you have to negotiate again for the best rate. Many mortgage brokerage lenders do not have posted rates, so you are guaranteed their lowest rates whenever you lock in.

Mortgage: A lien on the property that secures the promise to repay a loan.

Mortgage Banker: A company that originates loans and resells them to secondary mortgage lenders.

Mortgage Broker: A firm that originates and processes loans for a number of lenders.

Mortgage Insurance: A policy that protects lenders against some or most of the losses that can occur when a borrower defaults on a mortgage loan; mortgage insurance is required primarily for borrowers with a down payment of less than 20 percent of the home's purchase price.

Mortgage Modification: A loss-mitigation option that allows a borrower to refinance and/or extend the term of the mortgage loan and thus reduce the monthly payments.

Offer to Purchase: Indication by a potential buyer of a willingness to purchase a home at a specific price; generally, put forth in writing.

Origination: The process of preparing, submitting,

and evaluating a loan application; generally includes a credit check, verification of employment, and a property appraisal.

PIT: Principal, Interest, and Taxes—the three elements of a monthly mortgage payment; payments of principal and interest go directly towards repaying the loan, while the portion that covers taxes goes to the city for payment of property taxes.

Pre-Approve: Lender commits to lend to a potential borrower; commitment remains as long as the borrower still meets the qualification requirements at the time of purchase.

Pre-Foreclosure Sale: Allows a defaulting borrower to sell the mortgaged property to satisfy the loan and avoid foreclosure.

Premium: An amount paid on a regular schedule by a policy holder that maintains insurance coverage.

Prepayment: Payment of the mortgage loan before the scheduled due date; may be subject to a prepayment penalty.

Pre-Qualify: A lender informally determines the maximum amount an individual is eligible to borrow.

Principle: The amount borrowed from a lender; doesn't include interest or additional fees.

Real Estate Agent: An individual who is licensed to negotiate and arrange real estate sales; works for a real estate broker.

Realtor: A real estate agent or broker who is a member of the Canadian Real Estate Association.

Refinancing: Paying off one loan by obtaining another; refinancing is generally done to secure better loan terms (like a lower interest rate).

Rent-to-Own: Assists low- to moderate-income home-buyers in purchasing a home by allowing them to lease a home with an option to buy; the monthly payment is made up of the rent plus an additional amount that is credited to an account for use as a down payment.

Surveyor's Certificate: A property diagram that indicates legal boundaries, easements, encroachments, rights of way, improvement locations, and so on.

Title Insurance: Insurance that protects the lender against any claims that arise from arguments about ownership of the property; also available for homebuyers.

Title Search: A check of public records to be sure that the seller is the recognized owner of the real estate and that there are no unsettled liens or other claims against the property.

Underwriting: The process of analyzing a loan application to determine the amount of risk involved in making the loan; it includes a review of the potential borrower's credit history and a judgment of the property value.

ABOUT THE AUTHORS

JESSI JOHNSON is Canada's only realtor and mortgage broker featured on Oprah Winfrey's *Million Dollar Neighbourhood,* and personally manages more than half a billion dollars in mortgages.

KYLE GREEN is one of the go-to resources for financing investment properties in Canada and has been in the top 1 percent of mortgage brokers since 2011.

Both self-made millionaires thanks to their personal real estate investments, Jessi and Kyle are routinely sought after to share their expertise through writing and speaking engagements. Together their goal is to show you how to make money in real estate now and grow your wealth for the future.